How do we know there is a GOD?

and other questions inappropriate in polite society

answered by John Warwick Montgomery

DIMENSION BOOKS
BETHANY FELLOWSHIP, INC.
Minneapolis, Minnesota

ISBN 0-87123-221-9

DIMENSION BOOKS
are published by
Bethany Fellowship, Inc.
6820 Auto Club Road
Minneapolis, Minnesota 55438

Printed in the United States of America

For

DR. AL SCHMIDT
Lenoir Rhyne College

who, like Socrates, loves awkward questions

PREFACE

> "Religion and politics must not
> be discussed in polite society."
> —Dictum of popular etiquette

Ours is a tolerant society. As in earlier centuries, we have our fanatics, but we would not think of burning them. Fanaticism—unless of the healthy, secular variety displayed on the football field or at Woodstock—is an aberration which is supposed to disappear best if ignored.

> When Jesus came to Golgotha they hanged Him
> on a tree,
> They drave great nails through hands and feet,
> and made a Calvary;
> They crowned Him with a crown of thorns, red
> were His wounds and deep,
> For those were crude and cruel days, and human
> flesh was cheap.
>
> When Jesus came to Birmingham, they simply
> passed Him by,
> They never hurt a hair of Him, they only let
> Him die;
> For men had grown more tender, and they would
> not give Him pain,
> They only just passed down the street, and left
> Him in the rain.
>
> Still Jesus cried, "Forgive them, for they know
> not what they do,"

And still it rained the winter rain that drenched
    Him through and through;
The crowds went home and left the streets without
    a soul to see,
And Jesus crouched against a wall and cried
    for Calvary.

But ultimate questions continue to be asked whether society likes them or not. To repress questions about the meaning of life is simply to drive them deeper into the unconscious where they will trouble our spirit and disturb our dreams. Studdert-Kennedy's "Jesus crouched against a wall" is the bête noire in more troubled lives than we would be prepared to admit.

Why are religious questions frowned upon? Because they seem unanswerable, and thus productive of conflicts of opinion. Unlike questions in "factual" realms, religious queries appear to focus on personal likes and dislikes or uncritical prejudices. But suppose the belief that religion is "just a matter of opinion" were an even greater prejudice? Suppose God once really came to earth to answer man's deepest religious longings? Suppose, out of eternal love, He inspired prophets and apostles to record His will for man? Then religious questions would be not only the most significant of all, but in fact the most answerable of all.

This little book is predicated on that assumption. The author agrees with Prime Minister

Gladstone when, as a Christian, he wrote to Lord Rosebery in 1880: "I always admired Mrs. Grote's saying that politics and theology were the only two really great subjects." And not merely great: inevitable, etiquette or no. For the answers—or non-answers—we embrace will condition our very being and determine the path of our society. In the film version of *Cabaret*, the most frightening scene of all is one not of storm trooper brutality, but of sentimental idealism: conversions to the religion of National Socialism as the stirring voice of Nazi youth sings of patriotism. Religious questions are too important to answer mindlessly. If they cannot be ignored, would it not be best to bring them fully into the light of day? Perhaps our bête noire, on closer examination, will turn out to be the hound of heaven—or a unicorn who (like the Christ-symbol he is) will carry us into the very court of the High King.

* * * * *

Religious believers are supposed to make things easy on themselves by "answering" only those questions they themselves have asked. This criticism (classically expressed by Paul Tillich) probably does apply to many question-and-answer books written by religionists. Whatever the failings of the present volume, this is not one of them. In not a single instance did the author pose the question himself. The questions arose from two sources. Some of them were directed to the author and four other Protestant theologians of different persuasions (including death-of-Goder William Hamilton and the late Bishop James A. Pike) by an astute Roman Catholic.* The vast majority (some fifty-nine) were supplied by Keith A. Price, executive director of the Sermons from Science Pavilion in Montreal, Canada, and represent those questions most frequently asked by the two million English- and French-speaking visitors to the Pavilion since it first began operating at Expo 67.

Thus the reader of this book should not feel out of place. He is among two million persons who would rather confront ultimate issues than conform to the dictates of polite society. He may not be a Socrates—willing even to pay the price of hemlock for the right to ask uncomfortable questions—but he is well aware that "the unexamined life is not worth living."

JOHN WARWICK MONTGOMERY

Strasbourg, France
21 December 1972:
The Feast of Doubting Thomas

---

* Robert Campbell, O.P. (ed.), *Spectrum of Protestant Beliefs* (Milwaukee: Bruce, 1968).

4

Contents

1. How Do We Know There Is a God?

Do you *really* want to know? Be sure that you are not asking the question just to avoid *meeting* God! The philosopher Kierkegaard pointed out the danger of arguing God's existence in His presence. We know there is a God for three reasons: first, nothing in this world is able to explain its own existence; thus, there must be a God in order to explain the world in which we find ourselves. Secondly, you can't explain Jesus Christ unless God exists. When one of His disciples said to Him, "Show us the Father," Jesus replied: "Have I been so long with you and you don't know me?" (Jn 14:8, 9). Thirdly, your heart tells you there is a God; otherwise you wouldn't have asked the question. The Bible says: "The fool hath said in his heart, there is no God" (Ps 53:1).

2. Where Did God Come From, and What Did He Do Before the Universe Began?

Someone asked Saint Augustine this question in the 5th century. Augustine gave two answers in his *Confessions*. First, since God is the origin of everything, including time, it is meaningless to ask where He came from or what He did *before* there was a universe. Secondly, Augustine suggests that God may have been preparing a suitable punishment for those who ask such questions! But we can go farther: because God is three persons in one Godhead, and God is love, we know that He has been expressing that love from eterntiy. What has He always been doing? He has always been loving, and the Bible tells us that He loved us before the foundation of the world.

3. What Is God Really Like?

I liked the "dialogue" between Gabriel and God in *Presbyterian Life:*

Gabriel. I swear-uh-state unequivocally that some young theologians are saying that your Primordial Totality has metamorphosed into the epiphany of immanence.

God. What does that mean?

Gabriel. I don't know, but we've got Augustine working on it.

God. Is brother Beelzebub behind this?

Gabriel. Actually, it started when a philosopher named Nietzsche coined the phrase, "God is dead"—

God. What is he doing now?

Gabriel. He's just finished writing on the west wall, "I was wrong" three trillion times.

To claim that "God is dead" is to be at least three trillion times wrong, for if God did not exist the objector would not exist—would thus be in a very poor position to present his objection!

With the Nicene Creed—confessed by all true Christians, whether Eastern Orthodox, Roman Catholic, or Protestant—I "believe in one God, the Father Almighty, Maker of heaven and earth, and of all things visible and invisible."

Why do I believe in this God of the historic church? Because, as St. Paul well put it, "The invisible things of Him from the creation of the world are clearly seen, being

11

understood by the things that are made, even His eternal power and Godhead" (Rom 1:20). But the person of Jesus Christ is an even more powerful reason to back up the Psalmist's claim that it is "the fool" who "says in his heart, there is no God," for Jesus is simply inexplicable apart from the existence of the God He incarnated.

Granted, the church's statements about God are anthropomorphic; they could not be otherwise, since they are made by human beings, and since God entered the human sphere in Jesus Christ. But the issue is not whether they are anthropomorphic—the issue is whether they are *true*. One achieves exactly nothing (except perhaps ambiguity) by substituting phrases like Tillich's "Being itself" for the biblical descriptions of God. Indeed, as I have emphasized in my recent work, *The 'Is God Dead?' Controversy*, the obscurity and vagueness of much contemporary Protestant theology of the liberal variety has borne predictable fruit in the death-of-God movement. The God Hamilton and Altizer execute is the God of Tillich, Robinson, and Pike—not the God of biblical faith and historic Christian confession.

4. What Is Your View of the Trinity?

Affirms the Athanasian Creed (one of the three "ecumenical" creeds subscribed to by all orthodox Christians, East and West, Catholic and Protestant): "We worship one God in Trinity, and Trinity in Unity, neither confounding the Persons, nor dividing the Substance." A hard saying, perhaps, but I believe it with all my heart.

I believe it because (despite its ancient terminology) it offers the best available "construct" or "model" for interrelating the biblical descriptions of God as Creator, Redeemer, and Sanctifier. We already have noted that Jesus fully identifies Himself with the Father through His words, acts, and specific claims; Jesus also asserts that the Holy Spirit is "another of the same kind" (Jn 14:16, Greek text) as Himself, and in His final charge to His disciples He places Father, Son, and Holy Spirit on precisely the same level (the Great Commission, Mt 28:19). At the same time, the personal identities of Father, Son, and Holy Spirit are manifestly evident in Holy Writ, though God is "one" to all the biblical writers. Conclusion: "one God in Trinity in Unity."

The doctrine of the Trinity is not "irrational"; what *is* irrational is to suppress the biblical evidence for Trinity in favor of Unity, or the evidence for Unity in favor of Trinity. Our data must take precedence over our models—or, stating it better, our models must sensitively reflect the full range of data. A close analogy to the theologian's procedure here lies in the work of the theoretical physicist: Subatomic entities are found, on examination, to possess wave properties (W), particle properties (P), and quantum properties (h). Though these characteristics are in many respects incompatible (particles don't diffract, while waves do, etc.), physicists "explain" or "model" an electron as PWh. They have to do this in order to give proper weight to all the relevant data. Likewise the theologian who speaks of God as "Three in One." Neither the scientist nor the theologian expects you to get a "picture" by way of his model; the purpose of the model is to help you take into account *all* of the facts, instead of perverting reality through superimposing an apparent "consistency" on it.

The choice is clear: either the Trinity or a "God" who is only a pale imitation of the Lord of biblical and confessional Christianity.

5. If God Is Love and All-Powerful, Why Does He Not Bring Peace on Earth?

True love cannot exist without freewill. If a father were to shut up his child in a room and force him always to do right or take away all of the bad consequences of his doing wrong, he would show the very opposite of love. This would turn his child into a subhuman puppet. As painful as it is, we can only show love by advice and persuasion, never by tyranny. God wants us to have peace on earth, and He has promised that one day He will return to establish His Kingdom of peace. But, in the meantime, He will not dangle us like puppets on a string. It is our sin and self-centeredness that prevents peace, and He offers us His love and grace to make us new men with peace in our hearts and the strength to bring peace to others. But He won't force us to accept His gift of love. "Behold, I stand at the door and knock," says Jesus. "If any man will open the door, I will come in to him and sup with him, and he with me" (Rev 3:20). Have you opened the door of your heart to Him?

6. What Do You Believe About the Person of Christ?

There is an old joke about an argument between a Jewish and a Roman Catholic boy. The Roman Catholic boy boasted that he could enter the priesthood—and some day might even become pope. When his Jewish friend was unimpressed, the Catholic boy said: "Well, what do you want? You want me to become Jesus Christ?" The Jewish boy replied smugly: "One of our fellows made it."

This is exactly what I *don't* believe about Jesus Christ: that He was just an ordinary person who climbed up to Godhead. Jesus was not the ideal boy scout who spent a three-year ministry helping little old ladies across the Sea of Galilee. He was absolutely unique, for He was no less than God in the flesh, come to earth to die for the sins of the world. "No man hath ascended up to heaven," He declared, "but He that came down from heaven, even the Son of man" (Jn 3:13).

As a matter of fact, if you or I claimed for ourselves the things Jesus claimed for Himself, we would be carted off for an intensive period of shock treatment. Said Jesus: "I and the Father are one, He who has seen Me has seen the Father"; etc., etc. He forgave sin (thus exercising a divine prerogative) and was ultimately crucified on the charge of blasphemy. To try to make Jesus into a humanistic ideal instead of a divine Savior is to run counter to all the historical facts about Him.

The Church—Protestant, Orthodox, and Catholic—always has confessed a Jesus who was "very God of very God" as well as true man. As C. S. Lewis nicely put it in *The Screwtape Letters*, any other "Jesus" is a product of demonic perversion, not historical fact: "The documents say what they say and cannot be added to; each new 'historical Jesus' therefore has to be got out of them by suppression at one point and exaggeration at another, and by that sort of guessing (*brilliant* is the adjective we [devils] teach humans to apply to it) on which no one would risk ten shillings in ordinary life, but which is enough to produce a crop of new Napoleons, new Shakespeares, and new Swifts, in every publisher's autumn list."

7. Do You Believe in the Virgin Birth?

The Virgin Birth occurred as a historical fact. It is recorded in the same primary-source records that tell us of Jesus' public ministry, death, and Resurrection. There is not one whit of textual evidence that the Virgin Birth accounts are "later additions" to the New Testament documents—all of which, in the judgment of the world's foremost biblical archeologist, W. F. Albright, were written "between the forties and the eighties of the first century A.D. (very probably sometime between about 50 and 75 A.D.)." If the old Fosdickian canard is raised that the Virgin Birth appears only in two Gospels (Matthew and Luke), then one need only recall that the Sermon on the Mount *likewise* appears only in those two Gospels—but few people try to argue that it is unhistorical!

Agreed that God could have come into the world in different ways. But this isn't the question. The question is: How *did* He come into the world? To answer such a question, we must go to the historical accounts and allow them to speak.

Of course, what really bugs certain theologians about the Virgin Birth is the miraculous character of it. But one must face the fact that historic, biblical Christianity is a religion centering on God's miraculous intervention in the world. This advent was predicted through miraculous prophecy, and attested to by the miraculous creation of the Church by the Holy Spirit on the day of Pentecost (cf. Charles Williams' *The Descent of the Dove*). And the earthly life of our Lord was miraculous in its substance and in its culmination (the Resurrection). Why then boggle at His miraculous birth?

And if miracles get on our nerves, then we have Newtonian not Einsteinian nerves. For us, living in the wake of Einstein's revolution in physics, the universe is no longer a tight, safe, predictable playing field in which we know all the rules. Since Einstein, no modern has had the right to rule out the possibility of events because of prior knowledge of "natural law." Ironically, the theological demythologizers (who claim to be eminently up-to-date) are nineteenth- or even eighteenth-century "modern," for they live and think in a world where the Virgin Birth and the resurrection can be rejected *a priori*—apart from any historical investigation. Such a view is hopelessly unempirical and unscientific—to say nothing of being impossibly untheological. The New Testament writers, who had personal contact with the miraculous of Christ's life, were well aware of the distinction between myth and fact, and proclaimed the Virgin Birth as fully factual. "We," they write, "have not followed cunningly devised myths when we made known to you the power and coming of our Lord Jesus Christ, but were eye-witnesses of His majesty" (2 Pet 1:16).

8. Did Jesus Rise from the Dead? If So, How Do We Know He Is Alive Today?

Jesus' resurrection is one of the best attested facts in the history of the world. Eyewitnesses recorded His appearances over a forty-day period after He had been publicly crucified. In A.D. 56 Paul wrote to the Corinthians that the resurrected Jesus had been seen by over 500 people, most of whom were still alive. It takes more "faith" to disbelieve this evidence than to believe in it! We know Jesus is alive today because He said that He would return to the Father in Heaven, and His Ascension was likewise recorded by eyewitnesses. He promised, moreover, that He would come back to earth at the end of time in the same manner in which He ascended into heaven; when this occurs, "every knee shall bow and every tongue shall confess that Jesus Christ is Lord" (Phil 2:10, 11). People have only two choices: to confess Him as Lord now, voluntarily, or to confess Him whether they like it or not, and take the terrible consequences, on that dreadful day. How about you?

9. Is the Holy Spirit More Than a Mere Influence or Power?

According to Jesus, the Holy Spirit is, like Him, one of the three persons of the Godhead. The Spirit's work is twofold: (Jn 16:8). First, he "convinces the world of sin, righteousness, and judgment." In other words, He operates in history to convince men of their self-centeredness and their need for God's salvation. Secondly, He works in the hearts of believers as "the Comforter," applying the power of Christ to their lives. He is in every sense a person, having "brooded over the waters" at the creation, and praying today within Christian hearts the words which we do not know how to pray. Would you like this kind of comfort? Come to Jesus, and He will give you His Spirit.

10. How Reliable Are the Records We Have About Jesus?

Sir Frederic Kenyon, formerly Director and Principal Librarian of the British Museum and one of the foremost specialists on ancient texts in our century, wrote, shortly before his death: "The interval between the dates of original composition [of the Gospel records] and the earliest extant evidence becomes so small as to be in fact negligible, and the last foundation for any doubt that the Scriptures have come down to us substantially as they were written has now been removed. Both the *authenticity* and the general *integrity* of the books of the New Testament may be regarded as finally established." These records were in circulation when people who had known Jesus were still alive, and many of them were hostile to the Christian faith. It is inconceivable that the records could have distorted the true picture of Jesus without His critics blowing the whistle. The New Testament documents thus stood up in their own time, and have continued through the centuries to bring men into genuine contact with the real Jesus.

11. Is the Bible Really Inspired?

Is the Bible inspired? In a word, Yes! With all the great theologians of the Church history, today's Christian ought to hold that Sacred Scripture stands above all criticism and proclaims an absolutely veracious message to all men.

Said St. Augustine: "In an authority so high, admit but one officious lie, and there will not remain a single passage of those apparently difficult to practice or to believe, which on the same most pernicious rule may not be explained as a lie uttered by the author willfully and to serve some higher end." Likewise Luther, with his characteristically no-nonsense declarations: "The Scriptures have never erred" and "It is impossible that Scripture should contradict itself; it only appears so to senseless and obstinate hypocrites." The *Westminster Confession of Faith* took the same stand: "The Supreme Judge, by whom all controversies of religion are to be determined, and all decrees of councils, opinions of ancient writers, doctrines of men, and private spirits, are to be examined, and in whose sentence we are to rest, can be no other but the Holy Spirit speaking in the Scripture."

Why such a consistently strong biblical position on the part of Christendom's great theological spokesmen? Because the test of a great theologian is not his *originality*, but his *fidelity*, and the Augustines and Luthers of the Church have wanted to be entirely faithful to their Lord Christ in *His* approach to Scripture. When, at the beginning of Jesus' public ministry, the Devil quoted Scripture at Jesus in the wilderness, our Lord didn't say: "Oh, come now, we're too sophisticated for that sort of biblicism; let's get down to issues!" Rather, Christ did him one better—He quoted Scripture right back at the old evil foe, and capped it off with Deuteronomy 8:3: "Man shall not live by bread alone, but by *every word* that proceedeth out of the mouth of God." For Jesus, Scripture (the existing Old Testament and also the soon-to-be-written, apostolic New Testament—see Jn 14:26, and cf. 2 Pet 3:15-16) was totally and entirely God's word, and the Christian needs to view it in the same way. (And if he doesn't—if he criticizes it—he is really claiming to have a "revelation-to-the-second-power" which is capable of judging Scripture. But how could such a second-degree revelation be justified? And wouldn't *that* authority then require a revelation of the *third* power above *it*, and so on? here "Little bugs have littler bugs, and so *ad infinitum*?")

As for alleged contradictions and errors in the Bible, I like the observation of the Scandinavian theologian Valen-Sendstad: "It is remarkable that the nature of these so-called mistakes generally varies to correspond to the hearts and eyes that are contemplating them."

Moreover, the Bible is a clear and self-interpreting book, if we allow it to speak for itself. It requires no magisterium to tell us what it means, and, indeed, whenever a church or sect has set itself up as the authoritative interpreter of Scripture, the result invariably has been the obfuscation of God's word by fascinating but heretical human opinions. The story is told of a rather pompous cleric who gave his cleaning lady a big, fat, and learned commentary on the Gospel of John for Christmas. A month later he asked her if she was finding it useful. "Well, sir," she said, "at first I couldn't make head nor tail of it, but, you know, the Gospel of John has helped me greatly to understand it." Luther hit the theological nail nicely when he said: "The idea that in Scripture some things are recondite was spread by godless sophists who have never yet cited a single item to prove their crazy view; nor can they. And Satan has used these unsubstantial specters to scare men off reading the sacred text, and to destroy all sense of its value, so as to insure that his own brand of poisonous philosophy reigns supreme." Scripture, and Scripture alone, is the antidote to man's poisonous pastime of creating God in man's own image.

12. Why Should I Read the Bible If I Do Not Understand It?

The only way to understand it is to read it! Of course, the Bible is a library of sixty-six books, and some of them are easier to understand than others. The Old Testament is fulfilled in the New, so you can best understand the books of the Old Testament if you first read the New Testament books in which their meaning is made clear. Why not begin with the Gospel of Mark, the shortest of the Gospels and the one written specifically to introduce non-Israelites to Jesus' message? Or if you are a

Jew, why not begin with Matthew's Gospel, written expressly to show his Jewish contemporaries that Jesus fulfilled the prophecies of the Old Testament? If you are an "intellectual," start with Luke's Gospel, where the author is a physician concerned especially with the validity of Jesus' miracles. After reading either Matthew, Mark, or Luke, go to the Gospel of John, which gives the fullest interpretation of Jesus' ministry as recorded in the first three Gospels. Then read the rest of the New Testament, and use it as a basis for understanding the Old. You will be surprised to discover that the Bible is immensely easier to understand than the commentaries written on it.

13. Why Are There So Many Different Interpretations of the Bible?

Someone has said that you can get anything out of the Bible. This is true, *if* you are allowed to bring anything you want *to* the Bible. The many interpretations of the Bible are the result of our bringing our own ideas to the Bible and forcing the Bible to say what we want it to say. All branches of Christendom—Eastern Orthodox, Roman Catholic, and Protestant—find exactly the same central teachings in the Bible, for they all accept the same ecumenical creeds: the Apostles' Creed, the Nicene Creed, and the Athanasian Creed. The essence of these creeds is that God created man in His own image with freewill; man chose his own way rather than God's way, thereby ruining himself and his race; then God, out of infinite love, came to earth, taking man's penalty of death upon himself to free man from bondage. We can therefore be restored to a right relationship with God and with our fellow man by returning to God through Christ, even as the prodigal son returned to his father's house. You won't have any trouble discovering this message in the Bible; every passage breathes it.

14. Does Life Exist on Other Planets?

The best scientific opinion at present is that life in the sense in which we know it does not exist on any other planet of the solar system. There might of course be sentient life on the planets of other galaxies, but we have no way of knowing whether this is the case. If life does exist elsewhere in the universe, it has either remained in its primal love relationship with God or has fallen from grace as we have. If fallen, we can assume that God has given Himself for the salvation of those creatures in a manner as appropriate to their existence as was His death on the Cross appropriate to ours. If we were to visit an unfallen world, we would function as the serpent did in Genesis: we would offer the temptation of selfishness to creatures who had to that point lived selflessly. Is this perhaps why God has separated the worlds by such immense distances?

15. Isn't the Story of Creation Only a Myth?

Jesus didn't think so, and since He proved Himself to be God by His resurrection, He is presumably in the best position to make a judgment. He used the early chapters of Genesis as the basis for His teaching on marriage: He quotes the story of Adam and Eve as the basis for a man leaving father and mother and cleaving to his wife so that they become of one flesh. Since no human being was around when God created the world, no one is in a position to criticize the creation story in Genesis. Modern science continually changes its views on cosmology; this is inevitable, for science is reaching back to the origin of all things on the basis of much later data. Actually, if we realize that the word "day" is used in the Bible often to mean unspecified periods of time ("A day is with the Lord as a thousand years," Ps 90:4), it is not difficult to reconcile the "days" of Genesis with the geologic eras. It seems most likely that God created major species types throughout the geologic ages, evolution occurred in a limited way within individual

species types, and man was a special creation at the end of the creative period. This
accords with scientific fact, though it does
not go along with full-scale evolutionary
theory. But this is not strange, for scientific theory constantly changes, while "the
Word of God remains forever."

16. Can We Scientifically Explain Miracles?

A miracle is an unprecedented, unique
event. If by "explain it" we mean "account
for it as we do other events," this is impossible by definition. However, it is well to
remember that science cannot give ultimate explanations even of regular events!
The test of whether something happens is
not whether we can explain it. First we
must determine *whether* a thing happens;
then we will try to explain it if we can,
but if we can't, we still have to put up
with it. The evidence that biblical miracles,
such as the resurrection of Christ, really
happened, is as powerful historically as the
evidence for Caesar crossing the Rubicon
or Napoleon losing the Battle of Waterloo.

Let's not be like the old farmer who, on seeing a hippopotamus for the first time at the zoo and feeling at a loss to "explain it" because it was outside of his experience, refused to believe it was there.

17. If Christianity Is So Great, Why Are There So Few Christians Today?

Two thousand years ago, Jesus said: "Straight is the gate, and narrow is the way that leads to life, and few there be that find it" (Mt 4:17). In one of His parables, He suggested that only one quarter of the seed of His Word falls on good soil, producing fruit. Evidently, throughout history—not just today—only a few people come to Jesus. How come? Someone has rightly said that Christianity is the easiest religion in the world and also the hardest religion in the world. It is the easiest, because God, in His love, has done everything necessary for our salvation. It is the hardest, for we need to admit that we are entirely incapable of saving ourselves and need Him that much. It is our self-centeredness—our refusal to admit our need—that keeps us from Christ. What about you? Would you rather go with the crowd, maintaining the myth that you can solve your own religious problem, or are you willing to come to Christ on His terms?

18. What Impact Has Christianity Made During Its Two Thousand Years of Existence?

The greatest American historian of Christianity in our century, Kenneth Scott Latourette of Yale, produced a multivolume work, titled *A History of the Expansion of Christianity.* Says he of Christianity: "It was the main impulse in the formulation of international law. But for it the League of Nations and the United Nations would not have been. By its name and symbol the most extensive organization ever created for the relief of the suffering caused by war, the Red Cross, bears witness to its Christian origin. The list might go on indefinitely."

19. How Can Christians Say Their Religion Is the Only Way to God?

Jesus said: "I am the Way, the Truth, and the Life: no man comes to the Father but by Me" (Jn 14:6). Following what Jesus Himself thought, the Apostles preached that "there is no other Name under heaven," but the name of Jesus, "by which men must be saved." This is not to say other religions have no truth; but it is to say that unless those religions lead, directly or indirectly, to Christ, they mislead their followers into thinking that man can save himself apart from what God has done. Jesus also promised: "If any man is willing to do My will, he shall know of the doctrine, whether it is of God" (Jn 7:17). Missionaries have frequently told how, after preaching the Gospel to a primitive tribe, the people have said: "This is just what we were looking for." Sir Thomas More, in his classic, *Utopia*, said of the utopians that missionaries reached them because each night they prayed: "O God, if there is a religion high-

er and better than ours, may we hear of it."
Have you prayed that prayer?

20. Why Ask Me to Accept Your Religion? I Have One of My Own!

But is your religion one *you* have created
or the one that God has created? Water
can't rise above its own level; and self-
centered creatures can only produce religions that satisfy self-centeredness. We
need to recognize, in order to be saved, that
we can't save ourselves. Jesus said: "He
who would save his life shall lose it, but
he who would lose his life for My sake, the
same shall find it" (Mt 16:25). We need
to make sure that our religion is not a Tower of Babel which we build to try to reach
Heaven through our own efforts. We can't
do it, and if we try, the Tower will never
be completed and we will fall into total confusion. Said Jesus: "No man has ascended
up into Heaven. I have come down from
Heaven" (Jn 3:13). Why not get your religion from the only One Who brought it
from Heaven itself, and proved that He did
so by rising from the dead?

21. Don't All Religions Lead Us to God and to Heaven?

But the religions of the world contradict each other again and again in their teachings. They might all be wrong, but they certainly can't all be right! What about a religion of prejudice? or cannibalism? What about political religions such as Nazism or Marxism? What about religions that teach that we can save ourselves? We need "a more sure word of prophecy." We need a clear word from God to tell us whether a religious idea is a product of our own self-centered building of castles in air and when it is a genuine reflection of God's will. How to find out? Consider revelation claims. When a philosopher at the time of the French Revolution was unsuccessful in founding a new religion, Tallyrand said to him ironically: "Jesus, to found His religion, died and rose again on the third day. You could at least do that much!"

22. Who Is the Messiah? Is He Still to Come?

The word "Messiah" means "Anointed One." The expression is biblical, and refers to the Saviour whom God promised in the Old Testament to deliver His people. There have been a number of messianic claims in history. All but one came to nothing. For example, among false messiahs there was a certain Theudas, who promised in the year 44 that he would divide the waters of the Jordan River, and a few years later an unnamed "Egyptian" messiah gathered a crowd of 30,000 Jews and said that he would make the walls of Jericho fall down—but both incidents ended in complete failure, accompanied by bloodshed at the hands of the Romans. The one *proven* claim to Messiahship is that of Jesus, who said He would rise from the dead and did so. But does Jesus fulfill the Old Testament prophecies? A mathematician has analyzed the statistical significance of just 25 of the Old Testament prophecies Jesus fulfilled. His conclusion is that there would be but one chance in 33 million that all these foretold events would have come true if they were mere guesses or chance.

23. Why Are the Jews God's Chosen People? Isn't That Favoritism?

True, God chose the Jews as His own people out of all the nations. But He did so, not because of some kind of racial favoritism, but to show His glory. The Bible says that God chose "the weak things of this world to confound the wise." This choice placed a heavy burden on the Jews to follow exactly the revelation that God gave them, for "judgment comes first to the Jew." The Jews were given the incomparable privilege of being the vehicle for God's salvation through His Messiah; with that privilege of hearing God's word came a tremendous responsibility. The same is true for you, whether you are Jew or Gentile: what think ye of Christ?

24. Why Are So Many Christians Hypocrites?

How do you know they are? To be a hypocrite, a person must act differently from what he really believes. But how do you know that the man who doesn't act like a Christian really is one? "He is a church member," you say. But who ever said that all church members are Christians? A Christian is one who genuinely believes that God has saved him from his sins in Jesus Christ, and for whom Christ is more important than anything else. Jesus said that "the good tree brings forth good fruit"; true believers in Christ bring forth the fruits of Christ—and, anyway, even in the case of hypocritical church members, they are in a better place to be helped in church than they would be elsewhere, aren't they?

25. Is Not the Most Important Thing in Life to Love One Another?

Very definitely! But the problem is, how do we do it? Read the great love chapter in the Bible (I Corinthians 13), or compare your life with the life of the most loving person who ever lived, Jesus Christ. How do you match up? We all know we should be loving, but we just don't have it in us. When the chips are down, our selfish interests are more important than others. We need to become transformed people who *can* love the way we ought. But to achieve this ourselves is like pulling oneself up by one's own bootstraps. The love of Christ must come into our hearts. As the Bible says, we can only love on the basis of the fact that "He first loved us." To become loving, instead of just talking about it, accept Christ.

26. What Is Your View of Human Nature?

Sin did not destroy human nature. If it had, then God could not have become man to save us from our sin, for God then would have had to become a sinner. Moreover, if sin were basic to human nature, then human beings could never enter heaven, for the removal of their sinfulness by Christ's work on the cross would be the removal of themselves!

Contemporary existentialist theologians, as well as those, like Tillich, who have been much influenced by existentialism, have gotten into this kind of pickle by asserting that man falls "from essence to existence"—that Creation and Fall are really coterminous and equally necessary to the definition of man.

Actually, sinfulness is not the product of man's nature; it is the result of man's freely chosen misuse of his nature. God created man with free will, with the high privilege of choosing to serve God or to serve himself. As C. S. Lewis so effectively argued, love cannot be forced, and it must always accept the possibility of rejection. God, who is love, gave His creatures the choice of loving Him or not, and they, in choosing to be free of God, fell into a bondage of the most absolute kind. Said Jesus: "Truly, truly, I say to you, every one who commits sin is a slave to sin" (Jn 8:33-34). This bondage so conditions each subsequent generation that the choices open to the children of sinners become sinful choices within an already sinful context—and the race wanders in a labyrinth that has (humanly speaking, in Sartre's words), "no exit." The children of Adam have the freedom to choose their own poison, but not to perform curative operations on themselves. Only the Great Physician—Jesus Christ, who "was in all points tempted like as we are, yet without sin" (Heb 4:15)—can provide the remedy we need, for only He did not succumb to the disease. And in not succumbing, He displays what human nature properly is, and shows men the noble potentiality which God can actualize when sin's drag-effect is removed.

27. Is Man Not Able to Better Himself Morally by His Own Self-will?

The human race has not been very successful at this. The early 20th century French psychologist Emile Coué said that we could become better by repeating: "Every day, in every way, I am becoming better and better." But the horrifying wars of our own "century of progress" have shown that instead of becoming better, we have only become more efficient sinners. True progress! Six million Jews annihilated and Hiroshima! We just don't have goodness in us. We need Jesus Christ—every one of us.

28. Can I Be a Christian Without Going to Church?

You can *become* a Christian without going to church. After all, there wasn't any church when the Apostles became Christians just listening to Jesus. On the mission fields, people have regularly become Christians through the preaching of missionaries, even before a church was built. And many men have become Christians just by reading the Bible or by hearing the biblical Gospel from others. But once a man becomes a Christian, he won't be able to remain in isolation. Scripture says: "Do not forsake the assembling of yourselves together" (Heb 10:25). A Christian wants to be with other Christians, both to help them as Christ helped him, and in order to preach the Gospel to others more effectively. Said the church father Augustine: "It is not the absence of Baptism that damns, but the despising of Baptism." No man can despise the church and be a Christian.

29. Won't God Accept Anyone, Provided He Is Sincere and Does the Best He Can?

Suppose you have a severe headache, and go to the medicine cabinet to get some aspirin. You take some pills out of a bottle and swallow them, sincerely believing they are aspirin. They turn out to be deadly poison. Will your sincerity save you? Religion is a life or death matter, and there are many poisonous remedies under the name of religious answers. Sincerity is just not enough. You must be sure that what you sincerely believe in is *true*. You need to be sure that your religious beliefs represent God's truth. Go to the Bible, the only attested revelation, and you learn that our best is just not good enough. To enter a ballpark when the admission price is $1 is just as impossible if you have 50¢ as it is if you have only 10¢. People who say, "I am sincere; all I want on the Day of Judgment is what I deserve" will get exactly that—to their horror.

30. I Believe in *God*. Isn't That All That's Necessary?

Believing in God *is* all that's necessary IF you believe in the *right God*. But this is a mighty big IF. Theologian Paul Tillich frequently pointed out that there are almost as many gods as people who believe, for one's "god" is whatever one considers most important. Is your god your automobile? your job? your friends? your family? Even the gods of the many religions differ widely and contradict each other. The god of the Moslems considers women unfit for paradise. The gods of the Eastern Religions leave their followers at the mercy of agonizing reincarnation after reincarnation. Make sure you believe in the one true God. Said Jesus: "He who believes in the Father, believes in the One whom He has sent." And Jesus proved it, by His perfect life and resurrection from the dead. We need God *in Christ* because we need to be forgiven of our sins, and Christ's death on the Cross is the only way of forgiveness.

31. Why Do I Need Jesus Christ?

Jesus said that He came to earth "to seek and to save that which was lost" and to "give His life a ransom for many." Mankind—each of us—had gone his own way, rejecting God's standards and wallowing in selfishness, just like the Prodigal Son wasted his inheritance in a far country. Out of love for the fallen race, God came to earth in the person of Jesus, to take the death penalty man deserved upon Himself. When Jesus died on the Cross, He substituted for each of us, paying the penalty that we should have paid. You need Jesus because you need that penalty paid. Once He has taken away the penalty of your sins, the heavens open and you can come back into fellowship with God and man.

32. Will Those Who Have Never Heard of Christ Be Condemned?

The Bible makes perfectly plain the condition of those who have *accepted* Christ and the condition of those who have *rejected* Him. Those who have accepted receive eternal life; those who have rejected must pay the penalty of their own sins, for they have refused the only remedy for their disease. But the Bible leaves to God's mercy those who have never heard of Christ. Scripture says that no man comes to God except through Christ, but we do not know whether God may not have means of bringing Christ to people whom we have not been able to reach. Of course, we cannot assume that this will happen; and we are commanded to "preach the Gospel to every creature." If you are *really* concerned about this question, you will be more concerned to preach the Gospel to those who have not heard of Christ than to discuss the question theoretically!

33. What Happens Immediately After Death . . . Reincarnation?

The Bible says: "It is appointed unto man once to die, and after this the judgment" (Heb 9:27). Immediately after death, a man stands before the judgment seat of God, and God looks at him either in his self-centered condition or through Christ. The man who in this life depends upon Christ for salvation has Christ as his advocate on that dreadful day, and Christ's perfection stands in his stead. But the man who thinks he can save himself destroys himself because he cannot come to the level of God's perfection. There is no second chance. Reincarnation is supported neither by the Bible nor by scientific evidence. Don't take any chances. This is the only life you will have in which to accept Christ.

34. In What Sense Do Christians Have "Eternal Life" If Everyone Has an Immortal Soul?

Having an immortal soul means only *that* you will live forever; it doesn't tell you *where* you will live forever. The "eternal life" promised to Christians is life in the everlasting presence of Jesus Christ: a life characterized by all the wonderful qualities that Christ displayed while on earth—love, goodness, truth, beauty, and all the other perfections. But if a man rejects Christ, he chooses to separate himself from this kind of existence here and in eternity. He lives forever, but how monstrous the forever! Above all, don't make that mistake.

35. Do Heaven and Hell Really Exist?

Heaven is a place most certainly, for, though "no man hath ascended up to heaven," Christ "came down from heaven" (Jn 3:13) and told us that in His Father's house were many mansions. Indeed, Jesus said, "If it were not so, I would have told you" (Jn 14:2), the implication being that it should not even have been necessary to make the point with those who had committed their lives to Him. "The way ye know," continued Jesus: "I am the way, the truth, and the life; no man cometh unto the Father, but by Me." Heaven, then, is best characterized as the place where Jesus is. In a multi-dimensional universe such as ours, that "place" may be in our space-time continuum or it may not; perhaps, as a counterworld, it embraces our world at this very moment. We don't know; but we do know *that* it exists and that Christ has gone to "prepare a place" for those who trust Him with their eternal destiny.

Describing heaven is a very dangerous business, and the lady-angels and harping

saints of popular fancy frequently have re-
sulted in a throwing out of the baby (the
reality of heaven) with the bath water (the
unbiblical mythology). In contrast to this
sort of thing, I find especially helpful and
eminently scriptural the late C. S. Lewis'
stress on heaven in terms of *joy* and *depth*.
In *Surprised by Joy*, his spiritual autobiog-
raphy, Lewis described his lifelong search
for something beyond mere happiness: joy,
defined as an experience that one would
want repeated forever. That is heaven—a
condition (available in microcosm here and
now) which, because Christ is at its heart,
remains eternally fresh. In the last of his
seven Narnia Chronicles, Lewis pictures
the heavenly country as "world within
world, like an onion: except that as you go
in and in, each circle is larger than the
last." In those circles, the children find the
old mansion in which they first learned of
the land of Narnia, for there "no good thing
is destroyed." The new land was a "deeper
country"; as one new inhabitant expressed
it: "I have come home at last! This is my
real country! I belong here. This is the land
I have been looking for all my life, though
I never knew it till now."

Hell is as real as heaven, for it is as

clearly taught by Christ as is the reality of heaven. To pretend that hell doesn't exist or to rationalize it away accomplishes as little as putting one's head in the sand or ignoring the fact of cancer.

Heaven is where Christ is, where men and angels glorify Him and thereby become what they really are. Hell is where ego-centrism reigns, and fallen men and angels destroy their personalities by endeavoring to exclude Christ in favor of themselves. "He that findeth his life shall lose it: and he that loseth his life for My sake shall find it" (Mt 10:39). The exclusion of Christ means the exclusion of all good, since He is the source of all good, so hell is a terrifying condition to contemplate. But it is a condition which one creates for himself as he chooses to live apart from Christ; and the man who insists on running his own life in this world will obtain that horrifying privilege in the next.

Wrote W. H. Auden of Christian littéra-teur Charles Williams: "The popular notion of hell is morally revolting and intellect-ually incredible because it is conceived of in terms of human criminal law, as a torture inposed upon the sinner against his will by an all-powerful God. Charles Williams succeeds, where even Dante, I think, fails, in showing us that nobody is ever *sent* to hell; he, or she, insists on going there." Williams' description of the damnation of a woman who insisted on being her own god captures the essence of biblical teaching on the subject and ought to give us all pause: "She cried out, 'You thought you'd got me, didn't you?' They saw the immortal fixity of her constricted face, gleeful in her supposed triumph, lunatic in her escape, as it had at once a subdued lunatic glee in its cruel indulgence; and then she broke through the window again and was gone into that other City, there to wait and wander and mutter till she found what companions she could."

36. What Is "Sin"?

Someone has defined sin as the thing that causes us to look up our own name in the telephone directory as soon as it is delivered. This is not too inaccurate (though one would hate to give the impression that only bourgeois westerners with telephones are sinners), for it points up the

common element in all sinning: Self-centeredness and pride—the conviction that in the
final analysis we are the center of the universe. Lucifer convinced himself that he
was "like the most High"—and was
"brought down to hell, to the sides of the
pit." All sinful acts are attempts to set ourselves above God's will—to make ourselves
"the master of our fate and the captain
of our soul"—to engage in self-deification.
The inevitable result is the destruction of
a right relationship with God, and a corres-
ponding fracture of human relationships on
all levels—personal, national, and international.

In the nineteenth century, many persons
came to look upon sin as nothing more than
the unfortunate traces of earlier, less civi-
lized stages of human existence. It was argued that man could move forward to ideal-
istic perfection. Had not man improved
greatly since the barbaric Middle Ages?
Was not man making tremendous strides
in science, medicine, and the arts?

But the wars, both hot and cold, of the
last half century have shown that man, instead of becoming better, has only become
more efficient. He has managed to arrive
at the lofty pinnacle where he can kill

and maim more of his fellow human beings in less time than ever before.

And if we are honest with ourselves, we will admit that these identical tendencies exist in us. You haven't killed? Anger toward a fellow man is made of the same stuff, according to Jesus. You haven't committed adultery? "I say to you that everyone who looks at a woman lustfully has already committed adultery with her in his heart" (Mt 5:27-28). Liberal and radical theologians of our day who are trying to revive nineteenth-century optimism about man are doomed to disappointment, and their naïveté is appalling. Such views are possible only in those too young (or too senile?) to remember Verdun or Dachau— or too insensitive to see the face staring back at them in their shaving mirror.

37. What Is Meant by "Original Sin"?

This venerable doctrine generally is misunderstood, and the reason lies, I think, in the word "original." It does not mean that man "invented" sin (he can't even claim that for himself—Satan beat him to it!). "Original" is what Oxford philosopher Ian Ramsey calls a "sacral qualifier"—a word that points up the full dimensions of a religious truth. Sin is "original" in its *extensivenss* and its *intensiveness*. With the exception of Christ, all human beings have violated God's perfect will and the dictates of their own consciences. This was true of the first man and his progeny (whether he had long arms and scratched himself or not) and will be equally true of the last man (whether he will have an enlarged noggin or not). "All have sinned," says Scripture, "and have fallen short of the glory of God" (Rom 3:23).

In Genesis we read of man's original fellowship with God and his subsequent alienation—through self-interest—from his Creator. The Hebrew word *Adam* means man-in-general. It is the equivalent of the

Greek word that lies at the root of the English term anthropology. Anthropology is not the study just of Mr. A or Mr. B, but of man-in-general. Similarly, the Genesis account of the Fall deals not only with our first parents (and obviously we had some!), but also with all other men who have lived and who will ever live. "You should read the story of the Fall," said Luther, "as if it happened yesterday, and to you."

Original sin means, then, that we are all "east of Eden" (Steinbeck's novel nicely captures the essence of the biblical phrase). No one can sit in a house by the side of the road and watch the sinners go by. It is the fundamental pharisaic error to think that there is such a house. In point of fact, to use Beatnik poet Jack Kerouac's line, we are all "on the road," and the payment for that trip is established by a firm minimum-wage law: "the wage of sin is death" (Rom 6:23).

38. What Is the "Unpardonable Sin"?

This expression refers to what the Bible calls "the sin against the Holy Ghost." It consists of refusing to the end the grace that God offers through His Holy Spirit. The man who commits this sin keeps pushing away God's gift of salvation right to the point when it can do him no more good. He rationalizes away God's love and the gift of Christ, and refuses to believe that there are any eternal resources in the divine bank account on which the check of salvation has been drawn in his favor. Think of a airplane flying over the ocean; it can reach the "point of no return," after which there is not enough fuel in the tank to bring it back safely. Make sure that you do not pass this "point of no return" in your spiritual life. Remember: the longer you put off accepting God's offer, the harder it becomes to do so. "The same sun that melts the ice, hardens the clay." But as long as you are willing to respond to the Gospel, you have not committed the unpardonable sin.

39. Whom Will God Forgive?

Every man, without exception, who seeks forgiveness. There is no sin too great to keep a man from the Cross except the refusal to go to the Cross. Someone has rightly said that the only sin that ever damns is the sin of unbelief. "For God so loved the world, that He gave His only Son, that whosoever believes in Him should not perish, but have everlasting life" (Jn 3: 16). *You* are included in the "whosoever"!

40. What Must a Man Do to Be Saved?

Scene: The Admissions Desk, Heaven. *Characters:* St. Peter and Mr. Religious (a pillar of community and church for many years).

St. P: To enter here you must have earned 1000 points.

Mr. R: That doesn't seem excessive. I was a community leader for thirty years and strove for better government and general social improvement.

St. P: Excellent! A praiseworthy record. That's one point.

Mr. R (taken aback): I was a faithful family man—married to the same woman forty years and the father of three fine children whom we sent to the best schools . . .

St. P: You don't say? We don't get many like you these days. That's another point.

Mr. R (sweating freely by now): I was a scout leader, attended church every Sunday, was a member of the church board, taught Sunday School . . .

St. P: Commendable in every way! What a credit you were to the community. Two points. Now let's see, that makes . . .

Mr. R (on his knees, almost prostrate, half mumbling to himself): Good Lord! But for the grace of God, nobody could get in here!

St. P: You have just received 1000 points.

To be saved, a man must first recognize that he can't save himself. Why? Because everyone has willfully violated God's perfect standards, and he who "offends in one point of the law is guilty of all" (Jas 2:10). God's standard is perfection, as Jesus said in the Sermon on the Mount, and this means we all desperately need divine grace.

God's grace is given freely in Christ,

who died for our sins on the cross. This grace comes to us through the Word (the Bible) and the sacraments or ordinances (Baptism and the Lord's Supper), and we appropriate it through faith. This is the great truth of "justification by grace through faith" that the Reformers proclaimed on the basis of Scripture itself: "By grace you have been saved through faith; and this is not your own doing, it is the gift of God—not because of works, lest any man should boast" (Eph 2:8-9).

Faith, moreover, is not "the magic of believing" (as a book title has it). It is not faith-in-ourselves, or faith-in-faith. It is faith in *Christ*—the faith that cries: "God, be merciful to me a sinner." This never is mere intellectual assent. In the original Greek text of the New Testament "believe in Christ" literally means, "believe into Christ"—"enter into a living, personal relationship of trust with Him." The saved man is the man who (in Augustine's words) accepts God in Christ as the center and circumference of his life.

41. Does Having Faith Mean We No Longer Think for Ourselves?

Christian faith is not credulity. The Christian does not believe in spite of evidence, or even in the absence of evidence. For example, the historical data in support of the resurrection of Jesus Christ from the dead are greater than the historical evidence for Caesar crossing the Rubicon! Faith jumps the gap between probability and certainty. You experience this all the time in ordinary life: when you cross the street, it is faith that takes 100% of you across even though the evidence may be only 70% that you will not be hit by a car. As we have said before, faith is never mere intellectual assent. In the original Greek text of the New Testament "Believe in Christ" literally means, "Believe *into* Christ"—enter into a living, personal relationship of dependence on and trust in Him.

42. What Is the Relationship Between Faith and Good Deeds in Christianity?

No man can be saved by good deeds, for no one's deeds are good enough: all our deeds are tainted by self-centeredness, so they cannot satisfy the perfect demands of a holy God. Faith in Christ alone saves. "For by grace you have been saved through faith, and that not of yourselves; it is the gift of God, not of works, lest any man should boast" (Eph 2:8). But once a man has been saved by grace through faith, he does good works naturally—as a "good tree bears good fruit." This is what the Apostle James meant when he said that "faith without works is dead" (Ja 2:17). A person who claims to have saving faith and whose life is not Christ-like demonstrates that he does not have faith at all. Faith does not follow from good works; good works depend on faith.

43. Is Pre-Marital Sex Ever Legitimate?

In the little town in New York State where I grew up, there was one church that totally condemned dancing and most other forms of social contact between young people. The church was quite successful in this, except for one little difficulty: there were far and away more illegitimate births in that congregation than in any other church in the community! Why? (a) The pastor was so busy preaching against things the Bible leaves as open questions that his preachments against true immorality were lost in the shuffle. (b) The young people had nothing else to do. I look on that church situation as parabolic. If "pre-marital sex" means normal social contact between the sexes, then the Christian faith wholeheartedly approves. The kind of sex shibboleths characteristic of Bob Jones University are not only unbiblical; they are plain crazy and produce just the opposite effect from that desired.

But if pre-marital sex means intercourse before marriage, Christianity says No! unqualifiedly (the biblical word "fornication" refers in part to such activity). Situation sex is utterly un-Christian, for it violates the high analogy drawn in Scripture between Christ and the Church on the one hand and the faithful husband and wife on the other (Eph 5:22-32). To have intimate relations outside of marriage is the equivalent on the human level of idolatry on the spiritual level (1 Cor 6:13-20). When the late Bishop Pike, in such writings as his *Teen-Agers and Sex* (1965), gives existentially-oriented parents guidance in counseling teen-agers in the use of contraceptives and countenances abortion for pregnant teen-agers under certain "psychological circumstances," he prostitutes (and I use the word literally) his ministerial office.

44. Where Can I Find True Happiness?

As the philosophers have long realized, happiness can never be found by seeking it, for it is a by-product of the right kind of life. To seek it directly is like searching for the pot of gold at the end of the rainbow. This is why Jesus said: "He who seeks his life shall lose it, but he who loses his life for My sake, the same shall find it" (Mt 16:25). If you seek Christ, accept His salvation, and give your life to Him; happiness will come to you as a gift from God. "Seek first the Kingdom of God and His righteousness, and all other things shall be added" (Mt 6:33), promised Jesus.

45. How Can I Have Peace of Mind?

Ask yourself the hard question: Why don't I have peace of mind now? If you are honest, the answer will come back that the absence of peace of mind comes from insecurity—the agonizing fear that your life is not quite right, that a sudden turn of events could destroy it all. In other words, you are not sure of your relationship with the universe. Suppose you knew that you were right with God and that nothing could happen to you which would not be in accord with His perfect love for you; would you lack peace of mind then? You can have this assurance if you will come to God in the way He has set down in Scripture: by way of the Cross on which the Prince of glory died for you.

46. What Hope Does Christianity Hold Out to Men Today?

The same hope that it has always held out: the highest moral code on earth, the opportunity to become right with God and with one's fellow men, and the promise of eternal life in the presence of the Lord. Everything else changes, but God's promises always remain the same. Someone has said that the church proclaims "the unchanging Christ in a changing world." Precisely. The Bible says that "the Word of

God remains forever," and that "Jesus Christ is the same, yesterday, today, and forever." Don't you want the one secure hope in a world of hopeless confusion and change? Receive Christ today.

47. Are Edgar Cayce and Jeane Dixon Prophets of God?

Cayce was certainly *not* a prophet of God. His teachings are a mishmash of Eastern religiosity (karma and reincarnation) and out-of-context biblical teaching. Since his beliefs contradict the Bible, he cannot possibly be God's prophet. Jeane Dixon is a devout Roman Catholic, and certainly means well. But her prophecy that a child will be born who will unite all religions and bring peace in the year 2,000 can only be tied to biblical prophecy at the point of Antichrist. Mrs. Dixon can't be referring to Christ's Second Coming, for He will return directly from heaven. It should give us pause that the only other world leader in biblical prophecy is the Antichrist, and Mrs. Dixon looks positively on the birth of her religious leader. Is she a naive tool of evil forces?

48. Who and What Are Demons?

According to the Bible, demons are fallen angels—and they really exist. Through history, people who have had the temerity to call up devils or enter into pacts with them, like Faust, have discovered to their sorrow that they are real. For example, the great 19th century French novelist Huysmans was so frightened by the hellish phenomena he conjured that he ultimately became a Christian; said he: "Through a glimpse of the supernatural of evil I first obtained insight into the supernatural of God. With his hooked paw, the Devil drew me to God." Fortunately, there are better ways of coming to Christ than this!

49. What Does the Bible Say About Birth Control?

Scripture says that we should be as responsible about bringing another human being into the world as we are about our own lives. We should not be like the secularists, who consider children a matter of indifference to marriage; no Christian can take birth as lightly as the car sticker saying: "Trouble Parking? Try Planned Parenthood." On the other hand, the Bible does not remove responsible birth control from the decision of the married couple. They should recognize that children are normal to a marriage, but they should not permit the number of children to reach a point where they cannot be taken care of properly. As in all other areas of Christian life, such decisions should be made by faith and in prayer.

50. What Does the Bible Say About Abortion?

The Bible accords fully with the scientific fact that at conception the chromosomal father of the individual is entirely complete; Scripture plainly teaches that human life begins at conception. The human being does not come into existence at some later point. John the Baptist "leaped for joy" in his mother's womb. In a passage connecting childhood with God's Kingdom the word for child means literally "unborn child, embryo." Thus, from the biblical standpoint, abortion is homicide, and can only be "justified" as a lesser of evils. In certain circumstances, the death of the mother might be a greater evil than the death of her child, but one cannot assume automatically that this is the case. It is a sign of increasing paganism that we callously permit the killing of unborn children —genuine people who cannot defend themselves.

51. Is There Actually a Devil?

The great American evangelist Dwight Moody was once asked why he believed that the Devil existed. He answered: "For two reasons. First, because the Bible says so. Second, because I've done business with him." Moody was right on both counts. In fact, twentieth-century man has done so much business with Satan that not a few people (for example, some students I knew well at Cornell in my undergraduate days) find it easier to believe in the Devil than in God!

C. S. Lewis astutely wrote in the preface to his *Screwtape Letters*: "There are two equal and opposite errors into which our race can fall about the devils. One is to disbelieve in their existence. The other is to believe, and to feel an excessive and unhealthy interest in them. They themselves are equally pleased by both errors and hail a materialist or a magician with the same delight."

As the Church fathers recognized, however, Satan—who can never create, only pervert—frequently overplays his hand through pride. As we said before, the great *fin-de-siècle* French novelist J.-K. Huysmans so involved himself in satanic and occult activities that finally they convinced him of the reality not only of supernatural evil but also of supernatural good. Christianity is not a dualistic religion (like Zoroastrianism, for example) in which Satan exists on an equal plane with God; in the final analysis the Devil is, to use Luther's phrase, "God's Devil," and even his machinations are used against him in the councils of eternity.

52. Do I Have to Change My Religion to Become a True Christian?

"Religion" has never saved anybody. A man is not saved by being a Catholic or a Protestant; he is saved only by Jesus Christ. But someone has rightly noted that there are really only two kinds of religion in the world: those which teach that a man can somehow save himself (by dogmas, rituals, avoiding evil works, doing good works, etc.) and the Christianity of the Bible, which teaches that "all have sinned and come short of the glory of God" (Rom 3:23) and that "God commended His love towards us in that, while we were yet sinners, Christ died for us" (Rom 5:8). If you think you can save yourself, you had better change your religion, for it is really idolatry: you are worshipping yourself. If you are already connected with a Christian church, just make sure that you don't stop with the church, but allow it to carry out its proper task in your life, that is, point you to the Cross of Christ.

53. Aren't We Expected to Form Our Own Philosophy of Religion?

If the human race were still in Eden, in a perfect relationship with God, then there would be no trouble in formulating a philosophy of religion. But as a race we have preferred our selfishness to fellowship with God, and our "minds have become darkened," as Scripture puts it. The innumerable conflicting and contradictory philosophies of religion show how incapable we are of comprehending the universe. It has been well said: "Philosophy knows the questions, but unfortunately it doesn't have the answers for them." What we need is a religion from God—a clear Word from God—to tell us who we really are, who God is, and how we can be restored to a relationship with Him. The Bible is that revelation. Use your intellectual capacities, not in any illusory attempt to comprehend the universe philosophically, but in testing the veracity of God's Word. You will find that it withstands every criticism, and offers you the way to Life.

54. Should I Believe in Horoscopes?

If you do, you believe in something most unscientific. French astronomer Paul Couderc plotted the horoscopes of 2,817 musicians and found that there was no astrological relationship among them whatsoever. He concluded: "The musicians are born throughout the entire year on a chance basis. No sign of the Zodiac or fraction of a sign favors or does not favor them. The assets of scientific astrology are equal to Zero." Why not be like the Wise Men and let the Star of Bethlehem lead you to the manger, so that you can find your Savior there and worship Him?

55. Do People Really Communicate with the Dead?

The only case in the Bible of a communication with the dead should give us pause: King Saul went to the witch of Endor so that she would bring up the ghost of the

Prophet Samuel. This was the last stage of Saul's spiritual degeneration and madness. "Ghosts" can also be telepathic hallucinations, or the damned sent back to haunt the living, or Satanic counterfeits of the dead. Those who involve themselves in spiritism open themselves to the worst possible consequences: European psychiatrist Szondi has shown high correlation between occultism and schizophrenia. Don't play with fire—literally.

56. How Can I Overcome Depression?

First ask: Why am I depressed? Sometimes the reason is physical, and a physician can help. Sometimes the reason is psychological, and a counselor or psychologist can help. But often our depression comes from the nagging guilt of realizing that we are not the person we ought to be: we have fallen below our own standards; we have neglected our opportunities; we have prostituted our talents; we have not carried out our own ideals—to say nothing of God's.

This kind of depression is the first step to spiritual health, if it drives us to Christ. Says He: "He who believes in Me, though he were dead, yet shall he live; and he that lives and believes in Me shall never die" (Jn 11:25, 26). Spiritual depression is possible only when you are "pressed down" by the weight of your sin; let Christ lift you up eternally!

57. How Can Christianity Help a Lonely Person?

How can you any longer be lonely when you have a Friend who promises to be with you always? Says Jesus: "I will never leave you nor forsake you" (Heb 13:5). When you believe in Christ, you enter the fellowship of saints in heaven and on earth. You are surrounded by a "cloud of witnesses"; and you enter a church fellowship in which each believer "bears one another's burdens." Accept Jesus' everlasting friendship, and enter the company of the saints. There isn't any loneliness there.

58. How Can I Avoid Being Discouraged When Everything Goes Wrong?

If you have not given your life to Christ, there is no answer to such discouragement, for, apart from Christ, everything *does* go wrong! But with Him, everything goes *right*, according to the biblical promise: "All things work together for good to them that love God" (Rom 8:28). Not a single thing can occur in the life of a Christian which isn't best for him in the long run. We may not know why particular things happen to us, but God knows; only He has the perspective to see each event of our lives in relation to all the rest. But note the condition: this assurance is available only to those "who love God." And the love of God is not something we are capable of by our own efforts. God Himself sheds this love in our hearts when we believe in Him. Go to Christ, confess the sin of trying to run your own life, accept His salvation—and He will give you His Holy Spirit, who will kindle the flame of love in your heart and give you the wondrous benefits of His providential guidance.

59. What Do You Think About Divorce?

Jesus admitted only one valid ground for divorce—adultery (Mt 5:32—and there is not one whit of textual evidence that this passage has been doctored, *pace* the liberals). Malicious desertion is not a *ground* for divorce, it *is* divorce, so remarriage is legitimate for the deserted partner in such cases (1 Cor 7:15). But even in these sad cases, the ideal is to win the erring partner back, for a married couple are "no more two, but one flesh; what therefore God hath joined together, let not man put asunder" (Mt 19:3-6). As for the "burnt toast" variety of grounds for divorce permitted in some states and by some clergymen, Jesus would have had none of it.

On the other hand, it is important to note that the scriptural standards in these matters are set for *believers*. Because of the "hardness of hearts" Moses allowed a less strict divorce procedure and this received qualified approval from Jesus (Mt 19:7-9). Thus Christians ought to recognize that for unbelievers divorce and remarriage on non-biblical grounds may sometimes be the lesser of evils. But an evil it is, and it must not be rationalized as a good. The parties involved should be brought to see that such situations reflect our sinfulness and ought to drive us to the cross for God's forgiveness.

60. Do You Favor Racial Integration?

Racial integration is thoroughly Christian, for God created all men and Christ died for all men. The consequence is that "there is neither Jew nor Greek: ye are all one in Christ Jesus" (Gal 3:28). One of the greatest blots on the history of American churches is their toleration of the prejudicial treatment of minority races. No legitimate effort should be spared to help Negroes and other minorities to achieve full civil and social rights—and this requires direct opposition to unjust and immoral legislation (which, as a matter of fact, is not genuine legislation at all when it stands in opposition to God's eternal law!). "But, Dr. Montgomery, would *you* want *your* daughter to marry one of them?" "In a word,

Yes! Better that my daughter should marry a believing Negro than a bigoted White who has forgotten the love of Christ and 'passed by on the other side.' "

61. What About Anti-Semitism?

Anti-Semitism, and any other evil you can name, probably can be found in the life of some professing Christians. Why? I was recently reading an article by a scientist-who-is-a-Christian (one must watch the terminology here!), and he answered the parallel question, Why are so few scientists Christians? as follows: "For the same reason so few garbage collectors are Christian: *Sin.*" No one, except Christ, is perfect; Scripture declares: "If we say that we have no sin, we deceive ourselves" (1 Jn 1:8-10). But the Christian revelation, and Christ Himself, give no grounds whatever for justifying anti-Semitism. Indeed, in one sense the Scripture holds the Jew *above* the Gentile: because God's Word came through the Jewish nation, the "gospel of Christ is the power of God unto salvation to everyone that believeth, to the Jew first, and also to the Greek" (Rom 1:16, etc.). The unbelieving Jew today is a man caught in a kind of time-trap (to use science-fiction terminology); he is living in an unrealistic past, as if the Messiah had not come and the Dayspring had not dawned on high. The gentile Christian, recognizing that he himself is but a "grafted-in branch" on the tree of salvation, will try in love to point his Jewish neighbor to Jesus, who is at the same time the Jews' own Messiah and the Savior of all those who believe.

62. What Is Your Opinion of the Ecumenical Movement?

True, spiritual ecumenicity already exists among all Christians on the basis of their common relationship to the Lord of the Church, Jesus Christ. Organizational *union* (as compared with this already existing *unity*) is fervently to be wished for (compare Jesus' prayer, "that they all may be one"), but it must be pursued along proper lines. Union of churches is God-honoring only if it reflects agreement as to the contents of Christian truth. Mere emotional desire for a common Church ("ecclesiastical snuggling up") is not enough, and God's pure Word all too frequently has been obscured or lost in church unions producing more heat than light. (I like the comment about one big church that was created through ecumenical union of a lowest-common-denominator variety: "It's the church for those who don't care much for religion.")

Moreover, we Americans especially have to watch ourselves so that we don't bring into church life our favorite fallacy that "quantity makes quality." It is sobering to note that the modern ecumenical movement in the States gained its real momentum during the age of "big business" early in this century. Maybe the time has come for some anti-trust laws against some church organizations. It is just possible that gigantic churches can become as impersonal, inefficient, and productive of "organization-man" attitudes as any cartel. Frankly, I don't think that Parkinson's law ought to replace either the law of Moses or Christ's law of love. The way to true ecumenicity is to draw closer to Christ; in Him unimportant differences melt away and love for His truth becomes all-consuming.

63. What Is Your Reaction to Liberal Protestantism?

Protestant liberalism is the bane of theological existence, for it commits the worst sin of all: it stands in judgment on God's Word instead of letting God's Word proclaim judgment and grace to it. It creates God in the image of man's own rational faculties or subjective interests, rather than letting God create us in the image of His Son. To become *truly* liberal—truly free—one needs to be freed from sin and error by Christ; but this is exactly what the self-styled liberal refuses, in the interests of his supposed intellectual or moral autonomy. Like Marlowe's Faust, he becomes a law unto himself; and Scripture, not without reason, calls Antichrist "the Lawless One" (2 Th 2:8). The first step in salvation is to stop talking back and listen while God's Word does the speaking. Would that liberals learn this simple truth before they, in full clerical dress, cut off completely the limb they are sitting on, and fall ignominiously to earth, to the glee of the unbelieving world (a posture well illustrated by the ministerial anti-hero of Peter De Vries' novel, *The Mackerel Plaza*).

64. How Do You Feel About Roman Catholicism?

I cannot accept the so-called "Petrine theory": the theory that the true Church is that body maintaining a *successio personarum* (succession of persons) back to Peter as the first pope. For me, as for the Reformers, the only true succession is a *successio doctrinae* (succession of doctrine) which is determined by fidelity to Holy Scripture. Therefore I cannot accept the claims of the Roman Church, and I agree with Luther that, insofar as she proclaims that salvation involves man's cooperation with God (which is the exact opposite of the biblical teaching that salvation is by grace alone, as we have seen), she functions in the manner of an antichrist.

However, in practice, Roman Catholics in great numbers through the centuries have relied solely on the Christ of Scripture for salvation, and with the twentieth-century biblical revival in the Roman Church (stemming from the work of Père Lagrange and the École Biblique, etc.), more and more Catholics are bringing their religious life into line with the scriptural Word. (This does not, however, gloss over the sad biblical liberalism manifested by some "New Shape" Roman Catholic theologians, such as Jesuit John L. McKenzie.) Today Protestant liberalism and theological radicalism pose a far greater threat to historic Christian truth than does Rome. If I were forced to choose between them, I'd see my travel agent for a ticket to the Eternal City tomorrow.

65. What Are Your Convictions About Communism?

Christianity puts an imprimatur on no economic or political system. Neither capitalism nor communism, neither oligarchy nor democracy is "God's system." We do

the gospel a great disservice when we un-
critically identify it with "the stars and
stripes forever"—with our "American way
of life."

"Communism" (communal ownership
of wealth) is thus not to be condemned *per
se* by Christianity. But atheism is, and so
is totalitarianism (the subjugation of all life
and values to the state). Insofar as Russian
or Chinese communism is atheistic and to-
talitarian, *to that extent and for those reasons* it must be rejected as demonic. But
if (and it is a big if, admittedly) the Russian
state continues to exert less and less totali-
tarian pressure on its people, and *if* Marx-
ist theoreticians like Garaudy were to suc-
ceed in convincing the party that atheism
is not a necessary base for communist ideol-
ogy, then Christians would have no legitimate *theological* ground for blasting Russian communism. Hochhuth's play *The
Deputy* (whatever we may think of its por-
trait of Pius XII), points up the terrible
danger of viewing communism as the
worst of all evils, thereby allowing the end
to justify the means in opposing it—with
the result that even greater evils are per-
petrated.

Furthermore, there is something more

than a little disquieting in Jesus' teachings about not picking out specks in other people's eyes before extracting beams from one's own. Why, therefore, don't we American Christians devote some time to cleaning up our own capitalistic mess, where self-centered management tries to run rough-shod over government (remember the issue of steel prices?), where self-centered and corrupt labor leaders try to make everyone knuckle-under, even in time of war (Jimmie Hoffa inevitably comes to mind), and where all of us in a fat-cat economy justify our fat cathood in terms of individual initiative, while much of the world's population goes to bed hungry.

TOPICAL INDEX

90

Other Works by
John Warwick Montgomery

Published by Bethany Fellowship:

The Suicide of Christian Theology

Damned Through the Church

Situation Ethics: True or False? (with Joseph
    Fletcher)

Where Is History Going?

Christianity for the Tough-Minded

Principalities and Powers

Quest for Noah's Ark

Available from Other Publishers:

The Writing of Research Papers in Theology

A Union List of Serial Publications in Chicago-
    Area Protestant Theological Libraries

A Seventeenth Century View of European Li-
    braries

Chytraeus on Sacrifice: A Reformation Treatise
    in Biblical Theology

The Shape of the Past: An introduction to Phil-
    osophical Historiography

The 'Is God Dead?' Controversy

La Mort de Dieu (in French)

The Altizer-Montgomery Dialogue
    (with Thomas J. J. Altizer)

Crisis in Lutheran Theology, 2 vols.

History and Christianity

¿Es confiable el Christianismo? (in Spanish)

Ecumenicity, Evangelicals, and Rome

In Defense of Martin Luther

Computers, Cultural Change, and the Christ
    (trilingual: English, French, German)

Cross and Crucible, 2 vols.